HOW TIGER WOODS BECAME A MILLIONAIRE

SPORTS GAMES FOR KIDS
Children's Sports & Outdoors Books

Speedy Publishing LLC
40 E. Main St. #1156
Newark, DE 19711
www.speedypublishing.com

Copyright © 2017

All Rights reserved. No part of this book may be reproduced or used in any way or form or by any means whether electronic or mechanical, this means that you cannot record or photocopy any material ideas or tips that are provided in this book

If you are a fan of the game of golf, you know the name Tiger Woods. He is perhaps one of the greatest golfers of all time.

Read further to learn about his career and when he started playing golf, and how he got the name of Tiger Woods.

Golf Clubs.

ELDRICK TONT WOODS

Tiger was born on December 30, 1975 in Cypress, California and given the name of Eldrick Tont Woods. His father's soldier friend, nicknamed him Tiger, and the name stuck. Most people today know him by the name Tiger Woods. He was an only child for his mother, but has two half-brothers and a half-sister from his father's first marriage.

Tiger Woods hits a ball at Bethpage Black during the Barclays.

HIS EARLY LIFE AS A GOLFER

Tiger started playing at the age of 2. When he was 3, he was playing adult courses quite well. In fact, he was doing so well that when he was only 5, he was in Golf Digest, a golf magazine. At the age 8, Woods had won the Junior World Golf Championship playing against 9 to 10-year old's. He went on to win this championship 6 times!

He graduated in 1994 from Western High School at the age of 18 and became voted the *"Most Likely to Succeed"* by his classmates. He was a star for the school's golf team, coached by Don Crosby.

Tiger Woods waits to swing during practice rounds.

As a boy, he had to overcome stuttering difficulties. No one was aware of this until he sent a letter to a young boy that had contemplated suicide. In the letter, Tiger wrote, *"I know what it's like to be different and to sometimes not fit in. I also stuttered as a child and I would talk to my dog and he would sit there and listen until he fell asleep. I also took a class for two years to help me, and I finally learned to stop."*

American golfer Tiger Woods plays from the rough, third round at the Emirates Australian Open.

HIS COLLEGE GOLF CAREER

Woods chose Stanford University, even though he was recruited heavily by other colleges. He enrolled the fall of 1994 using his golf scholarship and went on to win his first collegiate event in September. His major was in economics.

When he was 19, he played in the 1995 Masters Tournament, his first PGA Tour, and was the only amateur to make the cut, tied at 41st. In 1996, at the age of 20, he was the first golfer winning three consecutive U.S. Amateur titles and also won the NCAA individual golf championship. He tied the amateur aggregate record with a score of 281 at the Open Championship, winning the silver medal. He decided to leave college and turn professional after two years. He left California in 1996.

Tiger Woods playing golf on Bosphorus Bridge.

HIS PROFESSIONAL CAREER

After turning pro in August of 1996, he immediately signed endorsement deals with Titleist and Nike, Inc. These were some of the most lucrative deals in the history of golf. Tiger was named as Sports Illustrated's Sportsman of the Year in 1996 and the PGA Tour Rookie of the year. He won the Masters in April of 1997, his first major win, breaking records and at 21, became this tournament's youngest winner ever. After a disappointing year in 1998, Tiger finished with eight wins during the 1999 season, which included the PGA Championship.

He went on to achieve six consecutive wins in 2000, which was the longest winning streak since 1948, accomplished by Ben Hogan. The 2000 U.S. Open was one of these wins where he either broke or tied nine records for the tournament, won by a 15-stroke record, and earned $800,000. When Tiger was 24, he became the youngest golfer to win the Grand Slam. By the end of 2000, Golf Digest ranked him as the 12th best golfer for all time.

Tiger Woods walking on the course.

He continued to master the game in 2007 and the beginning of 2008. He underwent knee surgery in April of 2008, missing the following two months on tour. His father passed away in May, and he took a hiatus for nine weeks. By the end of the season after his return, he was once again breaking records.

Hand putting golf ball on tee in golf course.

In 2009, he performed well, but failed to win a major. After his marital strife at the end of 2009, he decided to take an indefinite break from the sport. After the media coverage about his failed marriage, he delivered an apology. However, he lost many of his endorsements.

Man playing golf.

Tiger continued to play, but things no longer went as well as they had in his earlier career because of knee, elbow, and back injuries.

Woods' dominance reappeared in 2013 when, in January he won the Farmers Insurance Open, the 7th time he won this event.

He won the WGC-Cadillac Championship in March and two weeks later went on to win the Arnold Palmer Invitational. This win put him back at the top of the rankings and Nike soon launched an ad using the tagline *"Winning Takes Care Of Everything"*.

He started slow in 2014, he injured his back during the Honda Classic and was not able to finish. He struggled throughout tournaments during this year because of his injury.

Tiger Woods at the Emirates Australian Golf Open.

Again in 2015, he had to withdraw from a tournament because of his back injury. He returned to play at the 2015 Masters, finishing in a 17th place tie. He injured his wrist during the final round of this tournament. He played better at the Wyndham Championship, finishing four strokes behind the winner, tied for 10th place.

In 2016, Woods again sat out major tournaments while recovering from back surgery in September of 2015.

Tiger Woods (USA) practices at The Players championship, PGA Tour.

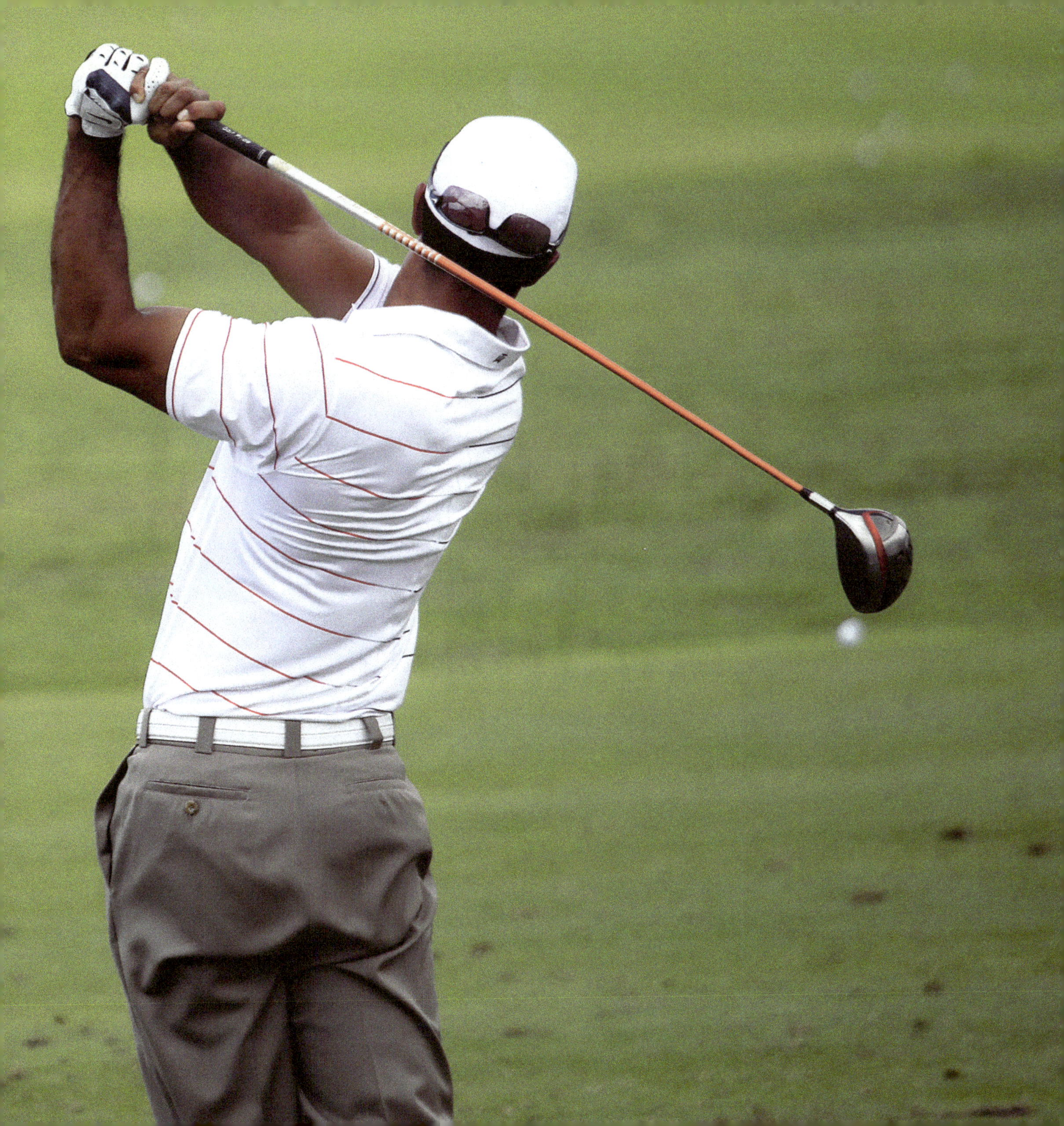

HIS PROFESSIONAL CAREER

Tiger was inducted into the California Hall of Fame on December 5, 2007.

In 2009 he was named as *"Athlete of the Decade"* by the Associated Press. He was named as the Associated Press Male Athlete of the Year four times, which is a record. Tiger is the only athlete to be named as Sports Illustrated's Sportsman of the Year more than one time.

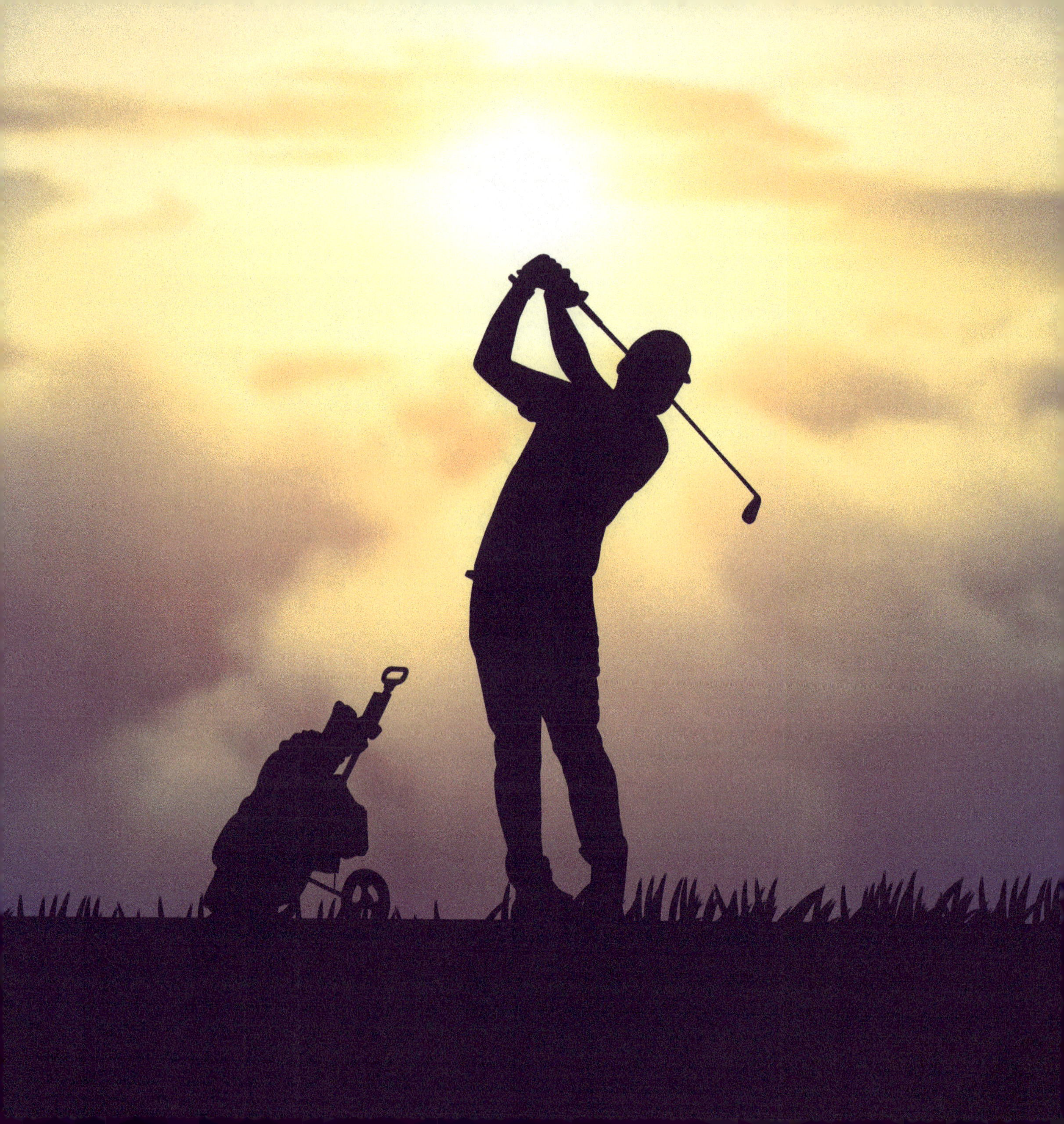

The increase is the popularity of golf is attributed to Tiger's presence in the game starting with his win at the 1997 Masters Tournament.

Silhouette of golfers hit.

HOW MUCH MONEY DOES HE MAKE?

He has done very well. He has made more money than anyone else on the PGA tour. He also makes a lot of money from his endorsement deals with Titleist, Nike, American Express, and General Motors. It was estimated he made over $100 million each year between 2007 and 2009.

Tiger Woods tees off the 12th hole on the Black Course.

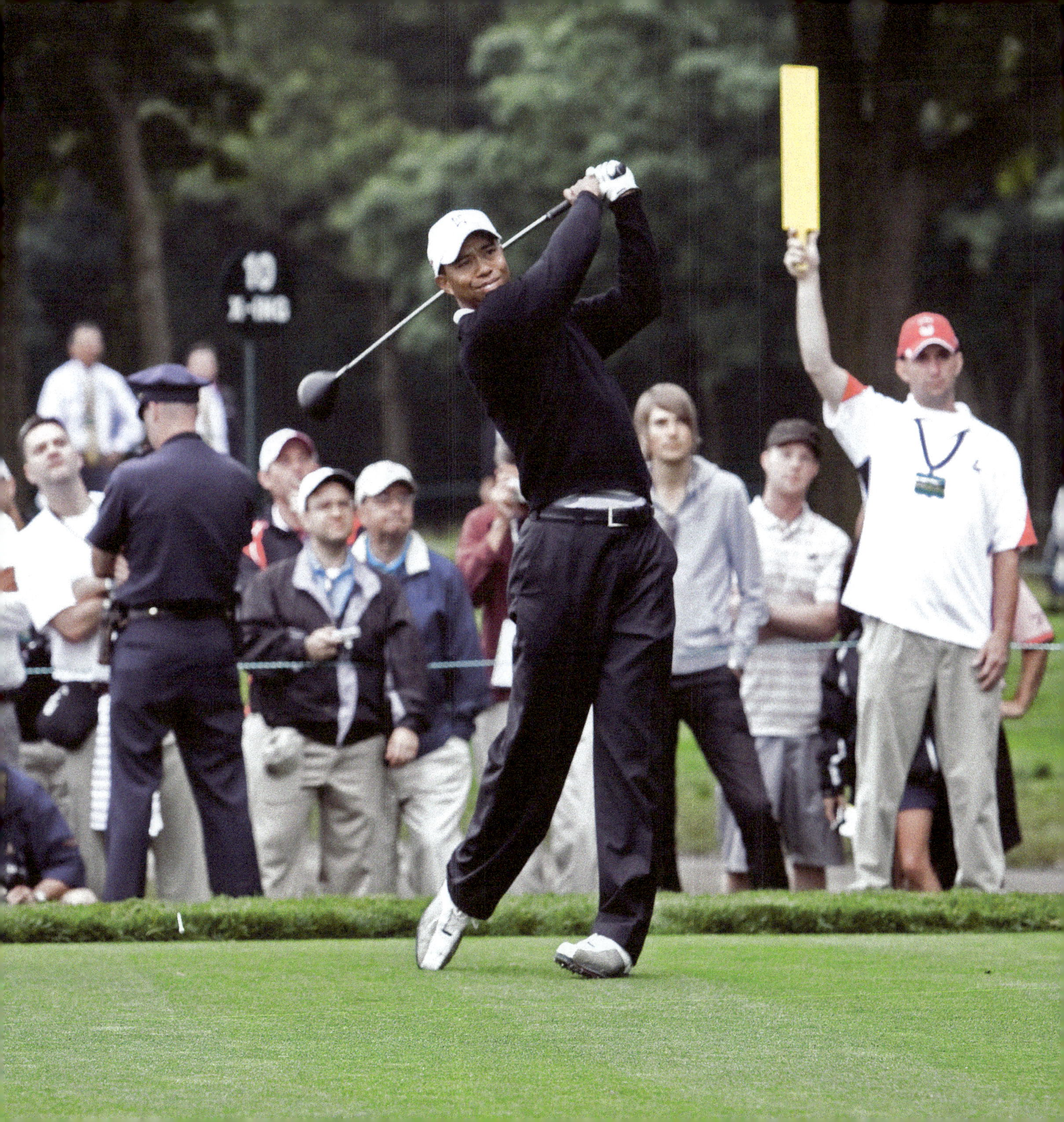
10

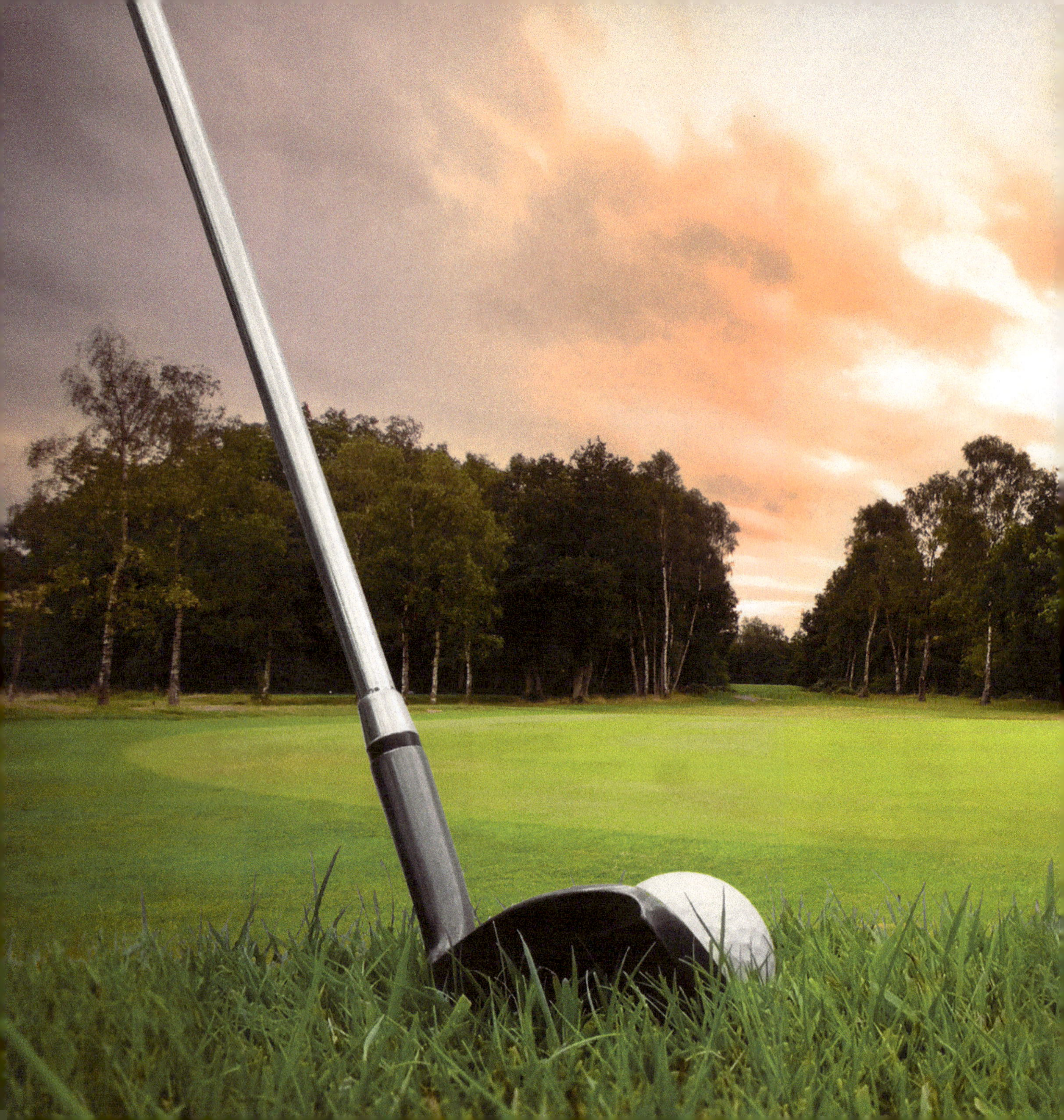

Chipping a golf ball onto the green.

ENDORSEMENTS

During the first ten years of his pro career, he was the most marketable athlete of the world. It was not too long after his birthday in 1996 he started signing deals with Nike, Accenture, American Express, General Mills, Titleist, and General Motors.

He signed a contract extension with Nike in 2000, which was a five-year, $105 million contract, the largest ever signed by an athlete. He receives a percentage of the sales of the Nike Golf brand, and had a building named for him at their headquarters in Beaverton, Oregon.

TAGHeuer

In 2002, Tiger became involved in all aspects when the Buick Rendezvous SUV was launched. His Buick contract was renewed in February of 2004, reportedly worth $40 million.

Woods worked closely with TAG Heuer for developing the first professional golf watch, which was released in April of 2005.

Tiger has also endorsed a series of video games called Tiger Woods PGA Tour since 1999. He signed a six-year extension in 2006 with the publisher, Electronic Arts.

The logo of the brand "Tag Heuer".

In February of 2007, he became the ambassador for *"Gillette Champions"* marketing campaign, along with Thierry Henry and Roger Federer. While the terms were not disclosed, it was estimated that this deal was worth between $10 million and $20 million.

Tiger Woods lines up a putt on the third green.

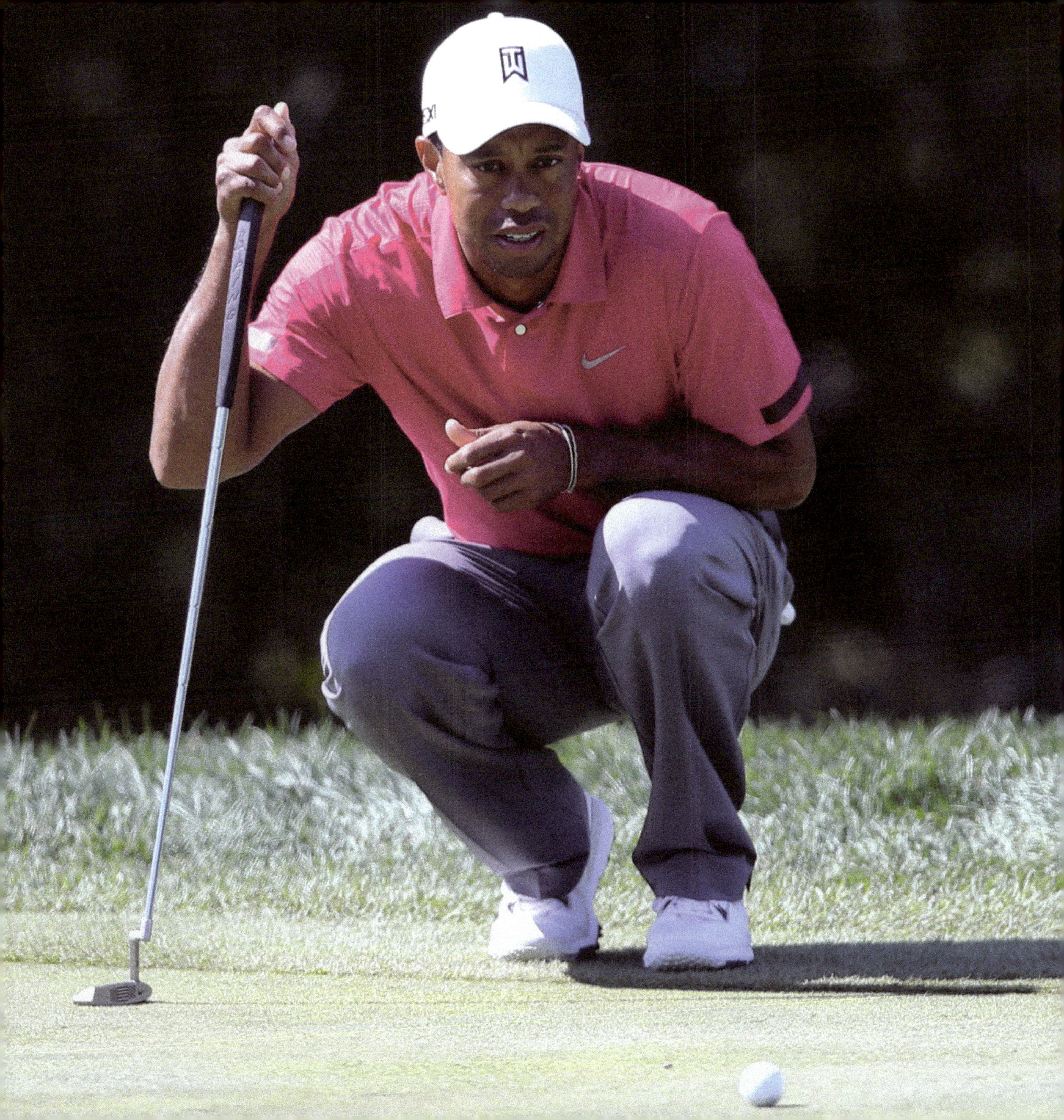

In October of 2007, it was announced by Gatorade that Tiger would have his own branded sports drink beginning in March of 2008. *"Gatorade Tiger"* became his first deal with a beverage company in the United States, as well as his first licensing agreement. It was reported that the deal was for five years and that he could make up to $100 million. Due to weak sales, the company decided to discontinue the drink in early fall 2009.

In July of 2011, he appeared in Japanese television commercial, 15 seconds long, as endorsement for a heat back rub by Kowa Co., referred to as the Vantelin Kowa rub. Details were never disclosed.

In October of 2012, an announcement was made that Tiger had signed an exclusive deal with a sports nutrition firm, Fuse Science, Inc.

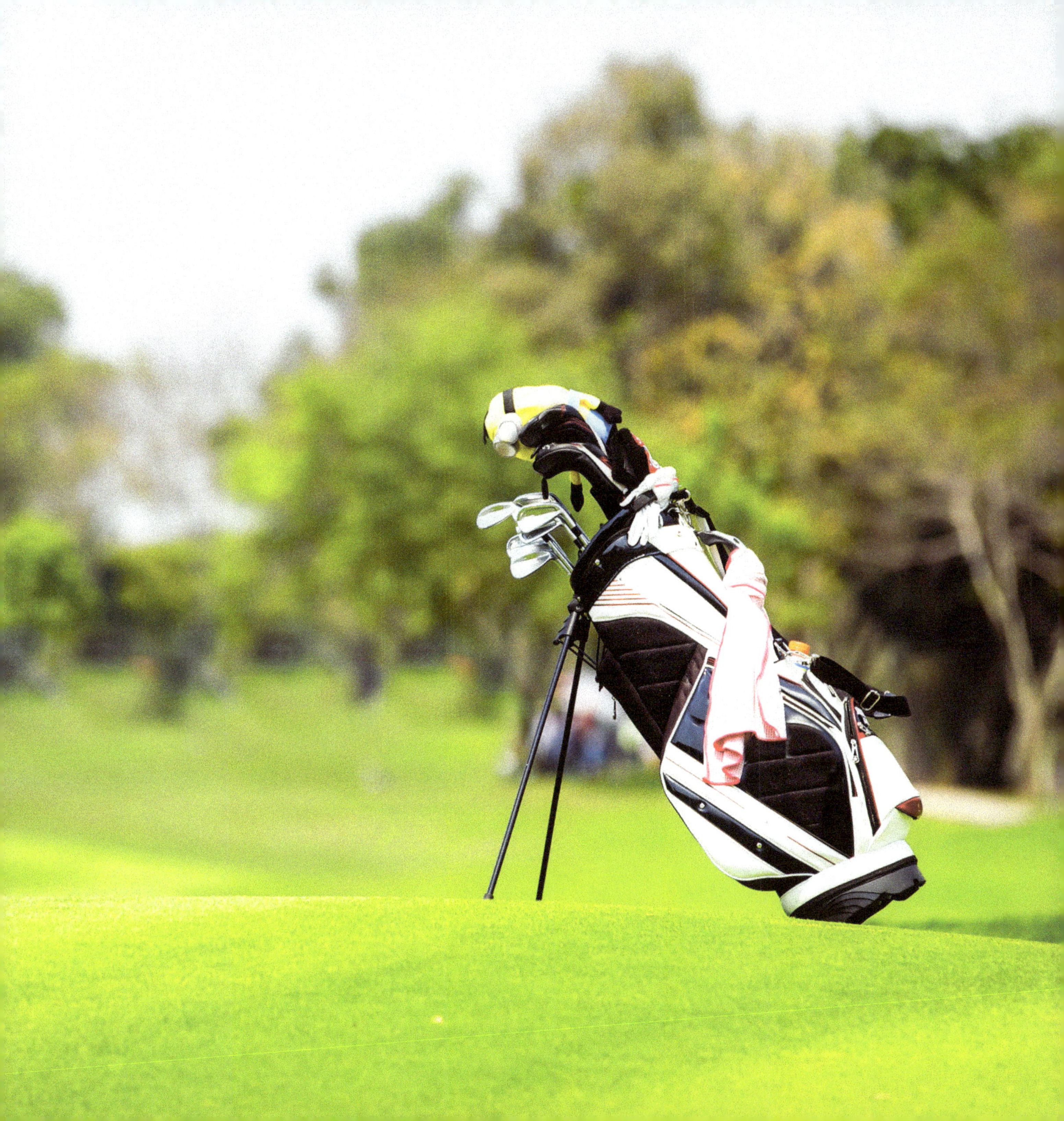

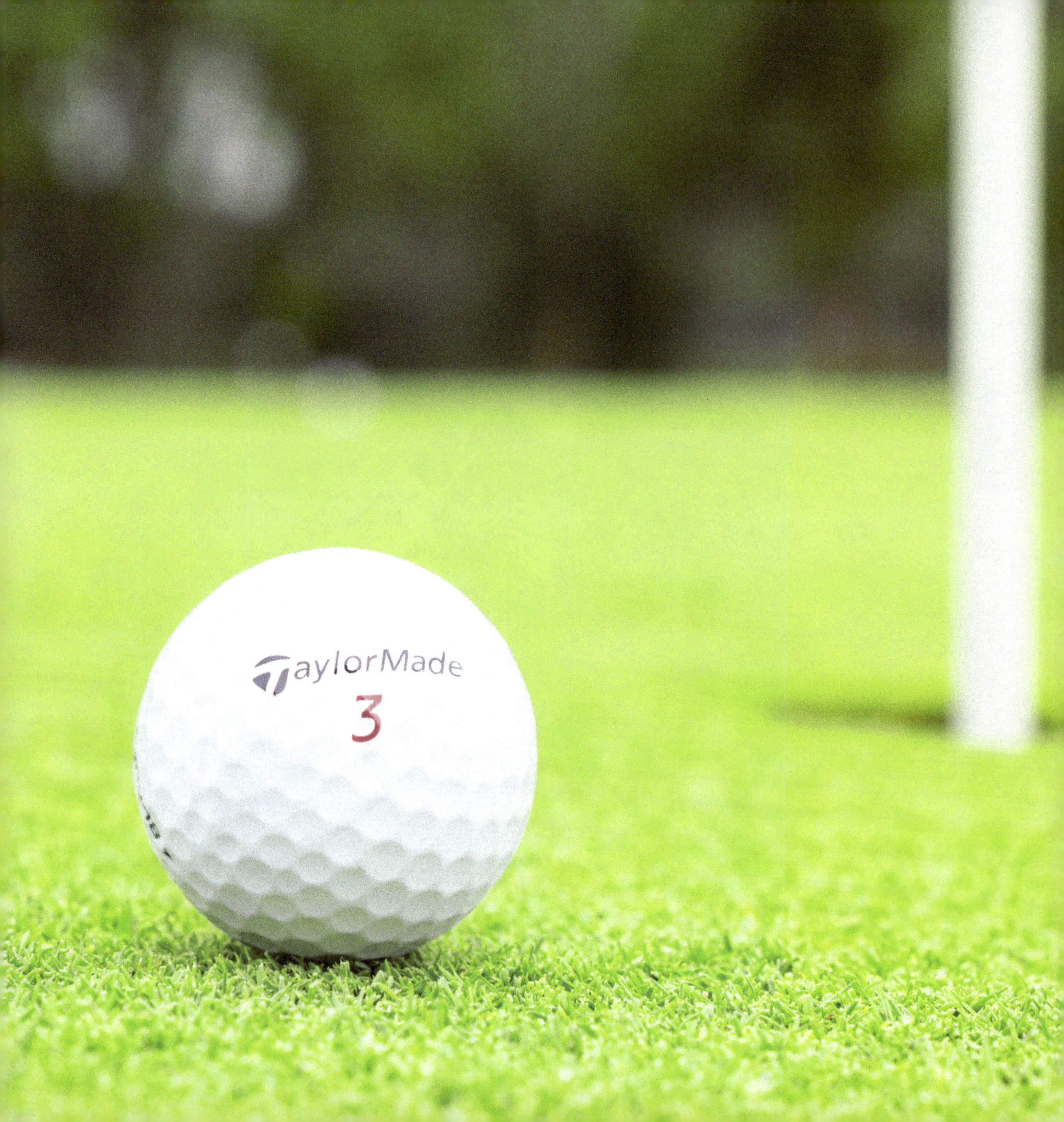
TaylorMade
3

Woods announced in August of 2016 that he would be searching for a new golf equipment partner after Nike left the equipment industry. On January 25, 2017, it was announced that Tiger would be signing a new club endorsement deal with TaylorMade.

A Taylormade branded golf ball on a green.

As you can tell, you can become a millionaire by playing great golf, but money from the endorsements continues, even after you no longer are playing the sport.

For more information about Tiger Woods, playing golf, or endorsements, you can take a trip to your local library, research the internet, and ask questions of your teachers, family, and friends.

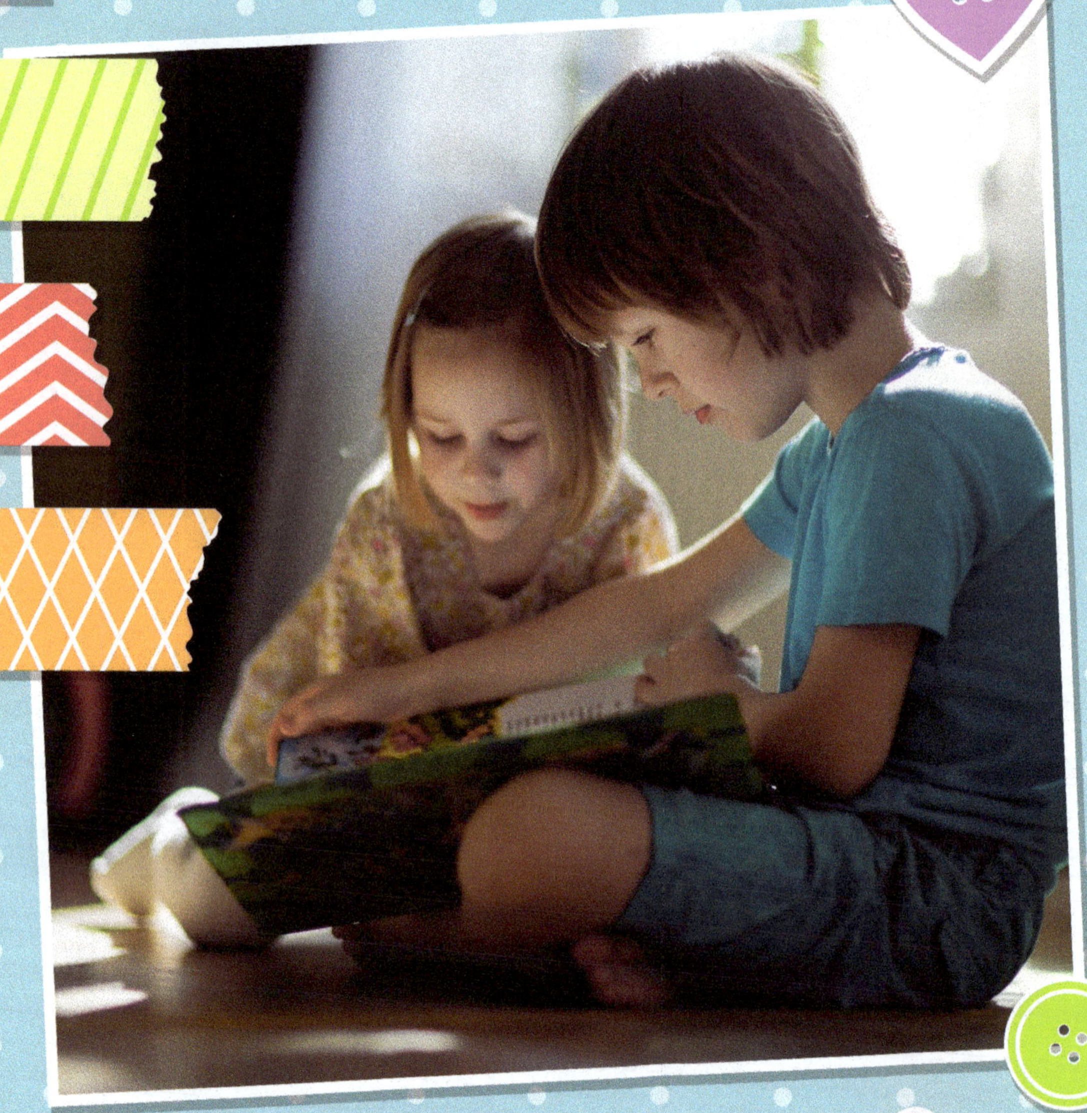

Visit

BABY PROFESSOR
EDUCATION KIDS

www.BabyProfessorBooks.com

to download Free Baby Professor eBooks and view our catalog of new and exciting Children's Books

Lightning Source UK Ltd.
Milton Keynes UK
UKHW051931250920
370548UK00005B/38